Recovery from Spiritual Bondage

Bishop John Kun Kun

Destiny House Publishing, LLC

P.O. Box 19774

Detroit, MI 48219

USA

www.destinyhousepublishing.com

inquiry@destinyhousepublishing.com

Artwork: © Can Stock Photo Inc. / Peter Denovo

ISBN-13: 978-1936867448

ISBN-10: 1936867443

DEDICATION

I dedicate this book to my Lord and Savior, Jesus Christ, who called me out of darkness into His marvelous light and gave me the wisdom to write this book.

This is also a dedication to my wife, Pastor Yvonne Kun, who gave me more encouragement to write.

I also dedicate it to my parents, John and Sharon Leiferman, who have given me all of the support to take my ministry worldwide.

CONTENTS

FORWARD

I have known Bishop John Kun Kun for almost two decades now and all along I have known him to be a very great revolutionary teacher of God's word.

We, his friends and admirers, usually call him Doctor, because of the grace of God upon his life to set captives free from spiritual bondage.

This book, "Recovery from Spiritual Bondage" is a masterpiece, because it talks about true freedom and recovery, as it deals mostly with building mental and spiritual capacity.

I recommend this book to anyone who wants to be mentally and spiritually liberated.

Rev. Elder Success K. Hopeson
President/ Founder
Glorious Kingdom Life Ministries Int'l.

PREFACE

The Word of God makes it very clear that the reason for bondage of God's children is their ignorance, lack of knowledge, rejection and despising of knowledge.

God's people are not destroyed because their enemies are stronger than they are, more skillful in battle than they are, smarter than they are or more powerful than they are.

My people are destroyed for lack of knowledge: because thou has rejected knowledge. (Hosea 4:6)

But the truth is that there are things the enemy knows about the authority, potential, principles and purposes that God has given to His people, that they do not know, or they are despising.

The enemy Is always happy when you don't know the things you ought to know, because it gives him an advantage over you. He has pleasure in your ignorance; for it leads you into the path of captivity that he wants you to walk in.

You can be an honorable captive if you lack knowledge and understanding. Your multitude can die of thirst in the midst of abundant water, all because of lack of knowledge. God didn't say in Isaiah 5:13 that the reason for their thirst was the lack of water; but rather, the lack of knowledge.

13 Therefore my people are gone into captivity, because they

have no knowledge: and their honourable men are famished, and their multitude dried up with thirst.

14 Therefore hell hath enlarged herself, and opened her mouth without measure: and their glory, and their multitude, and their pomp, and he that rejoiceth, shall descend into it.

15 And the mean man shall be brought down, and the mighty man shall be humbled, and the eyes of the lofty shall be humbled: (Isaiah 5:13-15)

I have often said to people in the many places I have ministered the Word of God, that prayer can release you temporarily and occasionally; but it takes the truth to give you freedom. Freedom is greater than release.

31 Then said Jesus to those Jews which believe on Him, If ye continue in my Words, then are ye my disciples indeed:

32 And Ye shall know the truth, and the truth shall make you free. (John 8:31-32)

Your freedom is guaranteed in the truth and not how many anointed men or prophets pray for you.

13 Whoever despises the Word and the counsel (of God) brings destruction upon themselves. (Prov. 13:13)

No matter who is praying for you or with you and fasting many days, as long as you despise the Word of Truth (God's instructions), you are sure to enter or remain in captivity. Your recovery from spiritual bondage is on the way, when you seek the Word of God, which is the truth.

CHAPTER 1
TRUTH ENCOUNTER

An encounter with truth brings you to the place of:

(1) Knowing your enemy, knowing his positions, knowing his strategies, and knowing what he has done and what he is capable of doing as a result of your lack of knowledge.

(2) Knowing yourself: This has to do with what the enemy has done to you and where he has kept you as a result of lack of knowledge. The reason for this is very simple. If you don't know what the enemy has done to you and how he has kept you in bondage, you will never desire and seek deliverance from that bondage.

(3) Having the knowledge of who God has made you in Christ, the position where He has placed you, and the authority He has given to you.

[5] They know not, neither will they understand; they walk on in darkness: all the foundations of the earth are out of course. (Psalms 82:5)

Until you encounter the truth, you will never ever understand what your enemy (the Devil) has done or is doing to you. Your foundation will be out of course. And if the foundations are destroyed, even the righteous cannot do anything about their destiny, their dreams, their future or their present crisis/situation.

^{3} If the foundations be destroyed, what can the righteous do? (Psalms 11:3)

Your foundation can only be in place when you have an encounter with the truth. Without the truth, you can never have understanding of many things that are wrong in your life. Understanding begins with knowing the truth. Walking in darkness can make you stumble. You might not even know the things that are hurting you in the dark. Based on this, you will be making assumptions of things that have caused you pains, bleedings, discomforts, wounds, tears and so forth.

In darkness you cannot see anything. Therefore, you will blame many things that are not responsible. All this happens because of lack of the knowledge of God's truth. It is revelation and enlightenment of truth that brings revolution and change.

The purpose of this book is to bring every reader out of the bondage that the Devil has kept them in all these years. Many are kept in the same cage their ancestors and parents have been in for centuries and decades. But I can tell you that by the eye-opening revelations in this book, you are coming out of whatever bondage that has kept you captive. No man departs from the path of captivity and bondage without a truth encounter (increased knowledge and understanding).

Lk. 15:11-28; The Prodigal Son's story

^{11} And he said, A certain man had two sons:

^{12} And the younger of them said to his father, "Father, give me the portion of goods that falleth to me". And he divided unto them his living.

¹³ And not many days after, the younger son gathered all together, and took his journey into a far country, and there wasted his substance with riotous living.

¹⁴ And when he had spent all, there arose a mighty famine in that land; and he began to be in want.

¹⁵ And he went and joined himself to a citizen of that country; and he sent him into his fields to feed swine.

¹⁶ And he would fain have filled his belly with the husks that the swine did eat: and no man gave unto him.

¹⁷ And when he came to himself, he said, How many hired servants of my fathers have bread enough and to spare, and I perish with hunger!

¹⁸ I will arise and go to my father, and will say unto him, Father, I have sinned against heaven, and before thee,

¹⁹ And am no more worthy to be called thy son: make me as one of thy hired servants.

²⁰ And he arose, and came to his father. But when he was yet a great way off, his father saw him, and had compassion, and ran, and fell on his neck, and kissed him.

²¹ And the son said unto him, Father, I have sinned against heaven, and in thy sight, and am no more worthy to be called thy son.

²² But the father said to his servants, Bring forth the best robe, and put it on him; and put a ring on his hand, and shoes on his feet:

23 And bring hither the fatted calf, and kill it; and let us eat, and be merry:

24 For this my son was dead, and is alive again; he was lost, and is found. And they began to be merry. (Luke 15:11-24)

The younger son thought he needed his portion of the father's wealth to be independent, successful and free.

In verse 13, He went to a far country because he didn't want anyone to influence or interfere with his life. Many times people think what they need are goods and great wealth to be happy and successful. But you will realize from here that because of the lack of knowledge and understanding, he gathered everything he had and wasted it all in one single verse.

It is more frustrating to have obtained wealth and then become a man in need, than to be a man managing his life without wealth.

After he had spent all, a famine arose and he began to want food, shelter and many other things for survival. He went to the point of eating swine's feed as his wages for feeding the swine. Can you imagine, the son of a rich man could stoop that low, because he lacked knowledge? He came from the place of abundance to barely surviving. He was at the mercy of another man who could not be compared to his profile. The problem was not the famine. Because while the famine was on, other people were employed, while he was seeking employment.

The portion he got from his father was bigger and greater than what the swine owner had. But yet in the time of famine, the swine owner became his employer. You can clearly and vividly see that the problem here was lack of knowledge and understanding of what to do with what he received from his father.

With knowledge, he would have invested it. But the Bible says he wasted it. Without knowledge a man can waste resources, talents, money, contacts, favor, and blessings from God. PRODIGAL was not his name, but because he was wasteful, that's what he was called.

The elder son, because of lack of knowledge, became jealous and angry at the younger one's return and the festival that was held for his reception.

[12] And the younger one of them said to his father, father give me the portion of goods that falleth to me. And he divided unto them his living. (Luke 15:12)

This means the elder son had his portion, but he did not celebrate it and couldn't make use of it. He was jealous of the younger one who knew what it meant to be the son of such a great man. Whenever you lack knowledge of your identity, your source, your authority and all that you have, you get involved in senseless battles and jealousies that lead to witchcraft.

Seek for knowledge that leads to an encounter with the truth which is by revelation of Jesus Christ himself. And then you are sure to recover from every form of bondage like poverty, sicknesses, witchcraft, occultism, marine powers etc. in Jesus' name.

CHAPTER 2
THE CAPACITY OF YOUR ENEMY

Your enemies, the Devil and his demons, have certain capabilities that you should not overlook. The Devil is a personality and not just a thing that you can treat carelessly. According to psychology, every personality is built on certain characteristics which include: will power, knowledge, emotions and the ability to speak.

Having this understanding will help you know the kind of enemy you are dealing with.

1. Your enemy the Devil has a will.

Matthew 12: 43-45;

[43] When the unclean spirit is gone out of a man, he walketh through dry places, seeking rest, and findeth none.

[44] Then he saith, I will return to my house from whence I came out; and when he is come, he findeth it empty, swept, and garnished.

[45] Then goeth he, and taketh with himself seven other spirits more wicked then himself, they enter in and dwell there: and the last state of that man is worse than the first. Even so shall it be also unto this wicked generation.

You can see from Matthew 12:44 how the enemy is expressing his will. His will is to bring seven more spirits more wicked than himself to increase your torment, sorrow, pains and your troubles. This means if you continue to walk in ignorance of his will you are in serious trouble as long as you continue on this earth.

2. Your enemy the Devil has a certain level of knowledge about you and the things that concern you.

Even though he is not omniscient (all-knowing) like our God, you need to understand that he has some depth of knowledge. When you are ignorant of his knowledge, he can cause you a lot of trouble, pain, sorrow, and calamities. He targets your divine purpose, destiny, health and assignment from God.

Mark 1:21-24;

21 And they went into Capernaum; And straightway on the Sabbath day he entered into the synagogue, and taught.

22 And they were astonished at his doctrine; for he taught them as one that had authority, and not as the scribes.

23 And there was in their synagogue a man with an unclean spirit; and he cried out,

24 Saying, let us alone; "What have we to do with thee, thou Jesus of Nazareth? Art thou come to destroy us? I know thee who thou art, the Holy one of God. (Mark 1:21-24)

You can see from Mark 1:25-27 that the Pharisees, the scribes and religious authorities who were in the synagogue did not know who Jesus was and the authority He carried. But the demons in Mark 1:24 said, "I know you, that you are the Son of the Holy God and that you have power to cast us out."

The leaders teaching the people in the temple did not know Who they were teaching about and the power that He had. But the demons had knowledge of Him and introduced Him to the religious leaders. That is why you need knowledge to deal with your enemy, the Devil. He is not an ignorant devil, neither is he a novice. He has been in battles many years with your ancestors and other people greater and more anointed than you. He also has history of the battles you are fighting right now. Therefore you need knowledge and understanding of a lot of things as you fight your enemy and his cohorts.

In Acts 19:15-16, the demons expressed to the sons of Sceva, a Jew and chief of the priests, that 'we are not ignorant. We have knowledge of spiritual authority; therefore we know who has the right to cast us out.' V:15. And the evil spirit answered and said, Jesus I know, and Paul I know, but who are You? V:16. And the man in whom the evil spirit was, leaped on them, and overcame them, and prevailed against them, so that they fled out of that house naked and wounded. (Acts 19:15-16)

"Jesus, I know and Paul, I know" means, I know their identities in God, I know their background and the authority they are clothed with. They have the power to cast us out but who are you? We know that you are fake and have not authority and power to cast us out. We even know your lifestyle, your greed for money, fame, and power, your immoral life and proud living, you cannot cast us out.

V:16; They became victims because they thought the enemy was ignorant and a novice in battle. Please understand that our warfare requires a lot of Biblical and spiritual knowledge in order to recover from spiritual bondage.

3. Your enemy the Devil has emotions.

Thou believest that there is one God; Thou doest well; The devils also believe, and tremble. (James 2:19)

This is one of the major characteristics of the Devil that makes him fight God's people. This characteristic of his emotions makes him envious and jealous of God's plans and purposes for our lives. He doesn't want to see God giving you and doing for you anything that he should have enjoyed, but missed because of his rebellion to God and God's plan for him. The Devil trembles when he hears the testimonies of what God is doing in and through you. He also trembles when he sees that, after he has done everything through your ancestors and parents by evil covenants and curses, you are still walking in the paths of success, prosperity, good health and righteousness. This makes the devil angry to declare war against you and your destiny and even your seed. Don't sit there and underestimate the capacity and potential of your enemy in warfare.

4. Your enemy the Devil has the ability to speak.

We see this ability in Mark 1:24 and Acts 19:15.

24 Saying, let us alone; what have we to do with thee, thou Jesus of Nazareth? Art thou come to destroy us? I know thee who thou art, the Holy One of God. (Mark 1:24)

15 And the evil spirit answered and said, Jesus I know, And Paul I know; Who are thee? (Acts 19:15)

This qualifies him to be the accuser of the brethren. If he is willing to accuse you falsely, how much more when he gets to know things that you are guilty of and have not yet confessed. He will use his speaking ability to destroy your boldness and confidence. He wants to halt your attacks on him and hinder you from doing whatever great thing you could have done in the kingdom of God. Please don't overlook or underestimate what the enemy can do to bring you shame and disgrace, and to hinder the promises and blessings of God in your life. Your recovery from spiritual, economic, financial, relationship and sickness bondage is based on your understanding of these spiritual revelations.

JOHN KUN KUN

CHAPTER 3
DEMONIC ENTRY POINTS

Everything going wrong in a man or woman's life is being controlled or influenced by one evil spirit or another. The devil is behind every oppression, depression, pain, disease, sickness and many other things that cause discomfort.

He doesn't operate until there is a legal ground given to him to perform and carry on whatever he wants to carry on. He will never have access into the lives of people until he finds legal ground to function, which I refer to as demonic entry points.

Let us go to the Bible and see what the Bible says about the entrance and functions of demons in the lives of people. This is a direct statement from the mouth of our Lord and Saviour, Jesus Christ, who is omniscient; that is all-knowing, which also suggests to us that He is also all-seeing.

[43] When the unclean spirit is gone out of a man, he walketh through dry places, seeking rest, and findeth none.

[44] Then he saith, I will return to my house from whence I came out; and when he is come, he findeth it empty, swept, and well garnished.

[45] Then goeth he and taketh with himself seven more other spirits more wicked than himself, then they enter in and dwell

there: and the last state of that man is worse than the first. And even so shall it be unto this wicked generation." (Matthew 12:43-45)

Jesus is giving revelation that evil spirits come into people and go out of people. They have points of entry that they use. If you are not knowledgeable of these things and have insight, you may become a perpetual victim of evil spirits, regardless of who is praying for you or with you, no matter how anointed and called they are. Sometimes even as a minister, when you are ignorant of this, you may have a person coming to you over and over again with the same condition and there is no change or improvement. Simply because after prayer or deliverance, they return and open the same door the enemy has been using to harass and torment them. Let us look at another revelation of this in Jesus' ministry while He walked here on the earth.

SOME DEMONIC ENTRY POINTS

1. Sin. John 5:14-15;

[14] Afterward Jesus findeth him in the temple, and said unto him, behold, thou art made whole: sin no more, lest a worse thing come unto thee.

[15] The man departed, and told the Jews it was Jesus, which had made him whole."

This man at the pool of Bethesda was impotent and had been in that condition and place for 38 years. Several efforts were made by relatives, friends, loved ones, religious leaders and everyone who sympathized with him in his condition to bring him out of it, but to no avail. Until the Master of Miracles, who knows all things, showed up and realized that this man didn't need a holy bath, anointing oil, or twenty one days of fasting and prayer. Instead, he needed mercy and forgiveness of his sin. It was a particular sin that brought that issue into his life. So Jesus had to let him know to stay away from that sin, so that a worse thing wouldn't happen to him.

There are many persons even in the kingdom today who, after receiving prayer or ministry, experience a certain level of release. After a short period, their case becomes worse than what it was before. This happens because they do not know that there is a particular sin that the enemy is using to return and afflict in a higher dimension.

I am not saying that all afflictions are caused by sin. Jesus made a lot of people whole without mentioning that it was their sin that made them sick. But there were also cases where sin was the entry point of their affliction and so sin had to be dealt with first, or they had to be cautioned not to return to such sinful acts. We can also see from another portion of scripture that Jesus had to forgive sin before healing.

⁵ When Jesus saw their faith, he said unto the sick of the palsy, son, thy sins be forgiven thee. (Mark 2:5)

They had faith enough for the paralyzed man to be healed: their faith became visible to Jesus and there was no doubt, but the healing was conditional in order for the entry point to be closed. Sin had to be dealt with in order to break the power of resistance that the affliction had. I know that **sin** is the root of every evil in the world, but I am not saying that the immediate cause of every torment, pain, infirmity, affliction or trouble is sin. What I am saying is that when sin is the immediate cause, until it is dealt with, the affliction will abide. When you are released and you don't know the cause of what afflicted you is a particular sin in your life, you will attract worse pain and afflictions from which you may not recover.

Like Jesus said to the man in John 5:14, there are even villages, towns, cities and nations that are faced with one kind of atrocity or another. Because of certain evils and sins that are dominant in the land, some lack development.

14 If my people, which are called by my name, shall humble themselves, and pray, and seek my face, and turn from their wicked ways; then will I hear from heaven, and forgive their sins, and will heal their land. (2 Chronicles 7:14)

Now you can understand that lands, nations, and cities can get sick and have a lot of problems because of the entry point of sin. There was another incident in John 9:1-3: Jesus' disciples thought (because of their little understanding) that the blind man became blind because of his sins or his parents' sin. Jesus was able to make clear to them that every affliction and sickness is not by personal or parental sins.

1 And as Jesus passed by, he saw a man which was blind from his birth.

2 And his disciples asked him, saying, "Master, who did sin, this man or his parents that he was born blind?

3 Jesus answered, neither hath this man sinned, nor his parents; but that the works of God should be made manifest. (Jn. 9:1-3)

Even though his problem was not his sin or his parents' sin, this reveals to us that SIN can also be responsible .

2. Unforgiveness.

John 20:21-23; When you refuse to forgive people who hurt you, it is said that it is like you are drinking poison and expecting the other person to die. Unforgiveness is a great open door for demons to occupy space in our lives. This can cause cancer, heart attacks, and many other illnesses to take residence in a person's body.

3. Brokenness and traumas.

When your life is broken and traumatized, demons can come and take over space in your life, if you are not careful. Many times this leads to self-pity. Then it becomes an opportunity for the enemy to draw closer to you and suggest to you. This can also lead to rejection which is one of the enemy's key instruments.

4. Evil generational, ancestral, parental, and personal covenants with evil spirits.

A covenant is a formal agreement between two or more people or nations; an obligation. A covenant is an agreement about an action to be taken. It is an accord, alliance, compact, convention, treaty and pact. A generational or ancestral covenant is a covenant or agreement that was entered into by your ancestors in order to achieve or accomplish a particular goal or purpose at that time for themselves or on behalf of the family, which causes a positive or negative impact in the life of members of the family. Let us take a look at a good example of an ancestral covenant that brought a positive result and blessings in the lives of generations in the past, present and generations to come.

² And I will make my covenant between me and thee, and will multiply thee exceedingly.

³ And Abram fell on his face: and God talked with him, saying,

⁴ As for me, behold, my covenant is with thee, and thou shalt be a father of many nations.

⁵ Neither shall thy name any more be called Abram, but thy name shall be Abraham; for a father of many nations have I made thee.

⁶ And I will make thee exceeding fruitful, and I will make nations of thee, and kings shall come out of thee.

⁷ And I will establish my covenant between me and thee and thy seed after thee in their generations for an everlasting covenant, to be a God unto thee, and to thy seed after thee.

⁸ And I will give unto thee, and to thy seed after thee, the land wherein thou art a stranger, all the land of Canaan, for an everlasting possession; and I will be their God.

⁹ And God said unto Abraham, Thou shalt keep my covenant therefore, thou, and thy seed after thee in their generations.

¹⁰ This is my covenant, which ye shall keep, between me and you and thy seed after thee; Every man child among you shall be circumcised.

¹¹ And ye shall circumcise the flesh of your foreskin; and it shall be a token of the covenant betwixt me and you.

¹² And he that is eight days old shall be circumcised among you, every man child in your generations, he that is born in the house, or bought with money of any stranger, which is not of

thy seed.

[13] He that is born in thy house, and he that is bought with thy money, must needs be circumcised: and my covenant shall be in your flesh for an everlasting covenant. (Gen. 17:2-13)

In this passage, we discover that the covenant Abraham made with God has several representations of the diverse kinds of covenants. Let us begin with this understanding that Abraham's covenant with God was a godly and positive covenant. This is only being used to show you the different levels of covenants. In this book, I want to put emphasis on negative and evil covenants; but the explanation of this will help you understand when I begin to deal with demonic covenants.

(a) It was Abraham who directly made the covenant with God; it was a personal covenant he made with God on behalf of himself. (Genesis 17:2-6)

(b) It was a parental covenant on behalf of his children and all who were in his house whom he served as guardian over and all who partook of the circumcision. (Genesis 17:7a, 13) "and thy seed after thee".

(c) It was an ancestral and generational covenant on the behalf of many of us who were not yet born or existing, but were yet to come to the faith of our Lord, Jesus Christ. (Genesis 17:7b) "and thy seed after thee in their generations for an everlasting covenant".

Gal. 3:13-15, Amplified Bible +;

[13] Christ purchased our freedom [redeeming us] from the curse (doom) of the Law [and its condemnation] by [Himself] becoming a curse for us, for it is written [in the Scriptures],

cursed is everyone who hangs on a tree (is crucified);

[14] To the end that through [their receiving] Christ Jesus, the blessing [promised] to Abraham might come upon the Gentiles, so that we through faith might [all] receive [the realization of] the promise of the [Holy] Spirit.

[15] To speak in terms of human relations, brethren, [if] even a man makes a last will and testament (a merely human covenant), no one sets it aside or makes it void or adds to it, once it has been drawn up and signed (ratified, confirmed). (Gal. 3:13-15, Amplified Bible +)

So, likewise, many people are victims of evil covenants that their ancestors and parents have made with evils spirits, witch doctors, fetish priests, cultic and occult groups.

This has made them victims in different aspects of life including: marriage, education, vocation, moral character and even social activities. Sometimes, people wonder why is it that they are making so much effort to succeed and progress in life and yet their lives cannot move forward, even though they applied much more seriousness, effort, time and strength than those who are getting better results and accomplishing more. But rather they see themselves going backwards in life and suffering so many setbacks. This is very frustrating. But I want you to know that many results in life are produced by the covenant that is serving as the foundation you are standing on or building upon consciously or unconsciously. Therefore, you need to check the covenant foundation that your ancestors or parents left for you to stand and build upon spiritually.

Please remember, it is the foundation that determines the size, height and durability of every building. And so when you refuse to examine your foundation before deciding what you want to build, no matter how fabulous and great your plans are, if your foundation is not in place or is faulty, your efforts and structure will crumble.

Covenant is one of the major producers of many things we see in our lives.

Lk. 13:11-16; Jesus did not boast in His power when a woman with an 18-year infirmity got healed. He attributed it to the fact that she was a daughter of Abraham and the covenant of Abraham brought her healing . Today Israel is still occupying that territory and is surrounded by enemies on every side but no one is able to remove them. Because of the covenant God made with Abraham in Genesis 17:7-9, Israel is not occupying and possessing that place because of military might but by reason of the covenant that God made with their ancestor and father Abraham .

5. Ancestral, parental, self-imposed and witchcraft curses.

Curse is defined by the Webster Dictionary as: an offensive word that people say when they are angry; magical words that are said to cause trouble or bad luck for someone or the condition that results when such words are said; a cause of trouble or bad luck; a prayer or invocation for harm or injury to come upon one; evil or misfortune that comes as if in response to imprecations or as retribution; a cause of great harm or misfortune; torment; to call divine or supernatural power to bring injury upon.

Let us look at another definition apart from Webster's dictionary. Curse is like a dark shadow that covers a person and hides their actual image or the glory that God has placed over them. Curse is like an evil hand from the past that is propelling one and making them to go the direction they do not desire in life and takes them out of purpose. Where there is a curse, it gives evil spirits room and permission to function in that territory or in a person's life. Curses can serve as entry points for evil (unclean spirits) to function in someone's life.

Curses cause dark spirits to accompany people, just as blessings can cause good angels to accompany good people to perform good things in their lives. Benediction is the opposite of curses.

No matter how strong, smart or skilful you are, a curse can close a mighty door of breakthrough before you.

Ancestral curses comes as a result of some things that your ancestors have done out of the will of God or evil covenants that they entered into. Sometimes they come by acts committed against innocent people. Likewise, parental curses come in a similar manner and also by negative words and evil pronouncements that parents speak over the lives of their children. E.g. Jacob's evil pronouncements over the lives of his children, Gen. 49:1-7;

[1] And Jacob called unto his sons, and said, Gather yourselves together, that I may tell you that which shall befall you in the last days.

[2] Gather yourselves together, and hear, ye sons of Jacob; and hearken unto Israel your father.

[3] Reuben, thou art my firstborn, my might, and the beginning of my strength, the excellency of dignity, and the excellency of power:

[4] Unstable as water, thou shalt not excel; because thou wentest

up to thy father's bed; then defiledst thou it: he went up to my couch.

⁵ Simeon and Levi are brethren; instruments of cruelty are in their habitations.

⁶ O my soul, come not thou into their secret; unto their assembly, mine honour, be not thou united: for in their anger they slew a man, and in their self will they digged down a wall.

⁷ Cursed be their anger, for it was fierce; and their wrath, for it was cruel: I will divide them in Jacob, and scatter them in Israel. (Gen. 49:1-7)

The above passage also reflects ancestral curses. What Jacob spoke also went down to generations for more than 400 years, calculating from the death of Jacob to the end of Moses' ministry.

Self-imposed curse comes as a result of things that are contrary to God's will and nature that you practice; and evil pronouncements and statements you make over your own life. Deuteronomy 27:15-26;

¹⁵ Cursed be the man that maketh any graven or molten image, an abomination unto the LORD, the work of the hands of the craftsman, and putteth it in a secret place. And all the people shall answer and say, Amen.

¹⁶ Cursed be he that setteth light by his father or his mother. And all the people shall say, Amen.

¹⁷ Cursed be he that removeth his neighbour's landmark. And all the people shall say, Amen.

¹⁸ Cursed be he that maketh the blind to wander out of the way. And all the people shall say, Amen.

¹⁹ Cursed be he that perverteth the judgment of the stranger, fatherless, and widow. And all the people shall say, Amen.

²⁰ Cursed be he that lieth with his father's wife; because he uncovereth his father's skirt. And all the people shall say, Amen.

²¹ Cursed be he that lieth with any manner of beast. And all the people shall say, Amen.

²² Cursed be he that lieth with his sister, the daughter of his father, or the daughter of his mother. And all the people shall say, Amen.

²³ Cursed be he that lieth with his mother in law. And all the people shall say, Amen.

²⁴ Cursed be he that smiteth his neighbour secretly. And all the people shall say, Amen.

²⁵ Cursed be he that taketh reward to slay an innocent person. And all the people shall say, Amen.

²⁶ Cursed be he that confirmeth not all the words to do them. And all the people shall say, Amen.

In subsequent books, when we shall be talking specifically about curses, we will give more details. But a few are listed above.

V:15; This is talking about any form of Idolatry or Idol worship.

V:16; This is talking about uncovering the nakedness which is the weaknesses of your natural parents and spiritual parents (e.g. Ham, the son of Noah. Gen. 9:20-23);

V:17; The scheming, cheating and crooked attitude of land dealers. This could also refer to moving of boundaries and spiritual laws that God had set into place. It is not good to tamper with or change them (e.g. claiming gay and homosexual rights). This is highly demonic and invokes curses on individuals and nations (Gen.19: Sodom and Gomorrah).

V:18; A tradesman, maybe a mechanic, who because his customers don't know about spare parts will take so much money from them and put another old part or something of less quality that will not function well. This invokes curses on people.

V:19; This is very clear in talking about people who prevent justice for those who are unable to defend themselves such as widows, orphans, etc.

V:20; Having sexual relations with your father's wife or your brothers/sisters. (e.g. Gen. 49:3-4; Reuben)

V:21; Having sex with animals (beasts) brings curse.

V:24; This is talking about using gossip to destroy your neighbor.

V:25; Taking a reward to destroy the innocent. There is no one as innocent as an unborn child. Therefore this includes abortion. Abortion brings a curse upon a woman and her womb that is been used as an altar to slay the innocent baby. The man that supports the abortion (morally and financially) also comes under the curse; this also includes the doctor and the hospital or place the abortion is committed.

This is why many hospitals are not saving lives as they should any more. This is also the reason why some houses are haunted houses.

There is a curse of not paying tithes and offerings: Malachi 3:8-11; Joel 2:25. When you refuse or fail to pay tithes and offerings, you attract devourers into your life and business. You will have to fight for yourself enemies that only God has the power to fight according to Mal. 3:11; He says, I will rebuke the devourer for your sake. But because you don't pay your tithes, you stay up all night praying useless prayers, worrying futilely. Your efforts are futile because you don't have the power to fight those enemies. Only God has that power and He can only move on your behalf against the devourers if you pay your full and complete tithes.

God calls the locust, caterpillar, canker worms and palmer worms His great army. That means He sends them for judgment on those who eat the tithe and offering. Pay your tithes and offerings and enjoy sweat-less living. Stop blaming witches and demons that are not responsible for your problems and struggles.

6. Visiting wrong places and people such as false and fake prophets, witch doctors, occults, etc.

Whenever you visit such places and people, you expose your spirit and entire being to another realm and atmosphere that is not good for you. You become vulnerable to all kinds of attacks and evil spirits.

Whenever you visit them, you surrender your authority and spiritual covering to them. You give them access to monitor and influence everything about your destiny. This wrong move also gives them the authority to manipulate everything about you; even the way you see things and people.

They can make you hate and turn against people that God will give you as destiny helpers and turn down opportunities and privileges that are for your good. By this means, they can afflict you at any time, mentally and physically. You have to be careful about the places you go to visit, and the people to whom you submit yourself.

1 Samuel 16:14-17 makes us understand that an evil spirit troubled Saul. And we also discovered that when Saul could not hear from God in 1 Samuel 28, he went to find a lady with familiar spirit in order to know what was trending in his kingdom. Perhaps, it was this practice that exposed him to evil spirits and their torments.

7. Pornography.

Looking at nude, naked and sexual photos and watching sexual movies leads to rape, murder and other violent acts. Pornography also promotes high levels of sexual immorality and unfaithfulness in marriages/relationships, masturbation, incest and other abusive acts.

8. Names. Gen. 25:20-26; 1 Chron. 4:9-10; Gen. 17:5;

[20] And Isaac was forty years old when he took Rebekah to wife, the daughter of Bethuel the Syrian of Padanaram, the sister to Laban the Syrian.

[21] And Isaac intreated the LORD for his wife, because she was barren: and the LORD was intreated of him, and Rebekah his wife conceived.

[22] And the children struggled together within her; and she said, If it be so, why am I thus? And she went to enquire of the LORD.

[23] And the LORD said unto her, Two nations are in thy womb,

and two manner of people shall be separated from thy bowels; and the one people shall be stronger than the other people; and the elder shall serve the younger.

24 And when her days to be delivered were fulfilled, behold, there were twins in her womb.

25 And the first came out red, all over like an hairy garment; and they called his name Esau.

26 And after that came his brother out, and his hand took hold on Esau's heel; and his name was called Jacob: and Isaac was threescore years old when she bare them. (Gen. 25:20-26; KJV)

From this passage of Scripture, you will discover that when Rebecca conceived and went to enquire of the Lord, the destinies of the children were revealed.

(1) It was revealed that they were going to be nations and not individuals.

(2) The elder would be stronger than the younger.

(3) The younger would be served by the elder because of the covenant God had with his fathers. Abraham and Isaac would be with him.

At birth, the destiny of the younger was tempered with a lot of challenges and delays, because of the name, Jacob, that was given to him. The name Jacob means *crooked person, supplanter, deceiver.* This alone changed his entire life from his original purpose. So many things that he was already entitled to from the womb, he had to deceive and trick people to get hold of them.

He didn't need his brother's birth right to get the blessing that God had already destined for him. He didn't need to wear goat skin and smell like a goat to receive his blessings.

He didn't have to miss out on the joy of being with his mother or get into trouble with his brother Esau, with his life being threatened. He did it all in the name of getting blessed. However, it was all because of the name that was given to him.

When Jacob encountered the Lord, the only setback that was discovered and needed change for fulfilment of his destiny was the change of his name. The moment his name was changed, destiny was restored and the brother that was hunting him to kill him could not harm him, but rather embraced him.

Esau was looking for Jacob but he met Israel, a man with a glorious destiny which he could not destroy. So he made an alliance with him.

[9] And Jabez was more honourable than his brethren: and his mother called his name Jabez, saying, Because I bare him with sorrow.

[10] And Jabez called on the God of Israel, saying, Oh that thou wouldest bless me indeed, and enlarge my coast, and that thine hand might be with me, and that thou wouldest keep me from evil, that it may not grieve me! And God granted him that which he requested. (1 Chronicles 4:9-10)

You may wonder, how can an honorable man pray such a prayer? All because things were not well with him. His life was experiencing so much sorrow in spite of the fact that he got his doctorate degrees and so forth.

The Bible makes us to understand that his mother named him

Jabez meaning *sorrow*, because of her own bad experiences and disappointments.

The honorable man had to pray for God to take away his sorrows, enlarge his tents and bless him. His name was his problem.

For Abraham to fulfil his destiny and God-given purpose as a father of many nations, God had to change his name also from Abram to Abraham and Sarai to Sarah. If names had no effect, why would God have to do that with His covenant people and even give Jesus a name as his reward in Philippians 2:6-11?

⁶ Who, being in the form of God, thought it not robbery to be equal with God:

⁷ But made himself of no reputation, and took upon him the form of a servant, and was made in the likeness of men:

⁸ And being found in fashion as a man, he humbled himself, and became obedient unto death, even the death of the cross.

⁹ Wherefore God also hath highly exalted him, and given him a name which is above every name:

¹⁰ That at the name of Jesus every knee should bow, of things in heaven, and things in earth, and things under the earth;

¹¹ And that every tongue should confess that Jesus Christ is Lord, to the glory of God the Father. (Philippians 2:6-11 KJV)

And God also give His Son the name that would fulfill His purpose as the SAVIOUR of the world.

³⁰ And the angel said unto her, Fear not, Mary: for thou hast found favour with God.

[31] And, behold, thou shalt conceive in thy womb, and bring forth a son, and shalt call his name JESUS.

[32] He shall be great, and shall be called the Son of the Highest: and the Lord God shall give unto him the throne of his father David: (Lk. 1:30-32)

9. Dreams that are used for entry points.

(a) Dreams of seeing yourself in former stages of life.

In this type of dream you find yourself often in your hometown or in the family home where you grew up; seeing yourself in school uniforms of schools you left many years ago.

These dreams can cause setbacks whenever you are doing your best to go forward in life. The enemy is revealing to you that no matter what you do, your life is going to manifest as if you are still living at that level or class of life that was seen in the dreams. Sometimes it is also revealing that there is a covenant or curse from your background that is manipulating you from progressing in your life.

(b) Dreams of frequent sexual intercourse, getting married, and having children in your dreams.

This can sometimes cause relationship problems, inability to get married, conflicts in marriages, frequent broken relationships. Frequent sex in the dreams can also cause incurable sexually-transmitted diseases and infections. This can also cause miscarriages, barrenness and impotency.

This also kills sexual desires between married couples. And it also leads to impotency in men. There are lots of people struggling with relationship problems. They don't even know that the dreams they are having are manipulating their relationships.

Marine agents also use this for initiation and spiritual defilements to cause disappointments, bad luck and unfulfilled promises.

(c) Eating in dreams.

Frequent eating in dreams can cause a lot of different situations but only a few will be mentioned for now. Eating in dreams can make one weak in their spiritual life. It destroys prayer life and makes one to over sleep and keep postponing their prayer time without praying at all.

Eating in dreams can also be used by witches to initiate people into witchcraft. Witches use the food as a point of contact in order to locate and monitor their victims.

Food in the dreams can also be used to afflict people with all kinds of sicknesses, diseases and infirmities. That is the reason why some people go to hospitals, meet with experienced doctors and specialists with advanced equipment and technologies and yet their cases cannot be diagnosed or treated.

Sometimes cancer, HIV, fibroids, diabetes, etc, can also be demonically transmitted to their victims.

(d) Buying and selling and receiving money in dreams.

This can frequently cause financial loss and business breakdowns or setbacks. The enemy uses this to do spiritual transactions with people and deny them profits and increases in whatever financial or business transactions they are involved with.

(e) Falling from heights.

This involves seeing yourself at a very high place and then of a sudden, there is a mysterious transfer to the ground or you see yourself falling from the high place.

When you are not conscious of the implications and cancel them by prayers using the blood of Jesus, it won't be long before you will find yourself lower at a level to which you never thought you would descend.

.

CHAPTER 4
DEALING WITH DEMONIC HORNS IN YOUR FAMILY

Zechariah 1:17-21;

[17] Cry yet, saying, Thus saith the LORD of hosts; My cities through prosperity shall yet be spread abroad; and the LORD shall yet comfort Zion, and shall yet choose Jerusalem.

[18] Then lifted I up mine eyes, and saw, and behold four horns.

[19] And I said unto the angel that talked with me, What be these? And he answered me, These are the horns which have scattered Judah, Israel, and Jerusalem.

[20] And the LORD shewed me four carpenters.

[21] Then said I, What come these to do? And he spake, saying, These are the horns which have scattered Judah, so that no man did lift up his head: but these are come to fray them, to cast out the horns of the Gentiles, which lifted up their horn over the land of Judah to scatter it. (Zechariah 1:17-21)

V:17; The Lord reveals His intention, purpose and desire to prosper His cities, comfort Zion and make Jerusalem His choice place. After He told His prophet to cry out loud and announce His divine plan, then rose up four horns to resist, hinder and confront this purpose and stop it from manifesting and coming to pass.

VV:18-19; Four horns were revealed to the same prophet to whom the Lord gave the mandate to make the declaration of His divine purpose. The mission and intention of the horns were made known to the prophet by the angel that spoke with him.

That mission was to scatter the nations and cities that God had already spoken about in order to ensure that the will of God for them would not come to pass. But rather, they should languish in ruin, shame, poverty and degradation.

It was also mentioned in verse 20, so that Judah will not be able to lift up his head. Meaning there will be no pride, honour or dignity.

VV:20-21; Talks about how God raised carpenters to fray the horns. The carpenters represent His own servants and forces to counter the mission and assignment of the horns. Praise God, I am one of His servants whom He has raised for this purpose and time. That is why I am speaking to you through this book to help you destroy those demonic horns that are standing against you and fighting your destiny.

According to Scripture, horns usually represent authorities and powers that be. These are powers that want to control and subdue people from fulfilling divine mandates and visions.

Horns can also represent demonic powers standing to make sure you are not fulfilled or accomplished. They are there to steal your joy and render you useless to your generation. But by God's grace, this will not be your portion because you are reading this book. Hallelujah! Say a loud "Amen!".

A demonic horn is any power that doesn't want your dreams, visions, aspirations, plans, destiny and divine purposes to come to pass.

Demonic horns are powers that try to suppress you, and make sure you do not gather anything. These demonic powers make sure you do not lift up your head, you are not established, and that you do not have peace and joy at any cost.

Let us look at the prophetic representations of the cities and nations that the four horns rose up against.

Remember, the demonic horns scattered Judah, Israel and Jerusalem. Judah means *praise*. The demonic horn wants to make sure you do not have praise in your life. Anything that will make your life praiseworthy or cause people to celebrate you, the horn comes to scatter them. The enemy wants to make sure you have no testimony that will bring you joy and praise.

Israel means *prince* or *ruler*. Therefore, the demonic horn wants to scatter your leadership ability, authority, and influence.

Whatever hinders you and doesn't allow you to attain a higher dimension in life is a demonic horn. Jerusalem means *city of peace*. The demonic horn is there to make sure there is no peace in your life and that you are surrounded by conflict and confusion.

The enemy's plan is to keep peace out of your family, marriage, ministry, business, vocation and any area that touches your life. He is there to scatter Jerusalem which represents your peace.

Dan. 7:21-22:

[21] I beheld, and the same horn made war with the saints, and

prevailed against them;

²² Until the Ancient of Days came, and judgment was given to the saints of the Most High; and the time came that the saints possessed the kingdom. (Daniel 7:21-22)

Prophet Daniel said he beheld the same demonic horns that were revealed to Zechariah in the past, that rose up against the nations and cities of Judah, Israel and Jerusalem making war against the saints. Remember, he said the same horn. Meaning the powers that are fighting you today to bring you down or render you useless, are the same powers that fought your ancestors and parents and made them into something that they are regretting and that you do not want to see in yourself.

Demonic horns are powers with long-time experience in battles in your family and generations. That is the reason why Jesus, as the Ancient of Days, had to confront and conquer Satan since he is the power behind the horns.

I want you to take notice that according to Daniel 7:21 the demonic horns fought against the saints like you and me and prevailed. So, it is not sufficient for us to sit and say we are children of God and not take the weapons (the blood of Jesus, the name of Jesus and the Word of God which is the sword of God) and use them appropriately according to the knowledge which we have received. We need to make war in Jesus' name against the demonic horns that have been standing against our generations.

CHAPTER 5
DEALING WITH BLOOD ISSUES

In preparation for finding and dealing with any evil in your family blood line, let us consider what Scripture says about <u>where</u> to look.

Lev. 17:11;

[11] For the life of the flesh is in the blood: and I have given it to you upon the altar to make an atonement for your souls: for it is the blood that maketh an atonement for the soul. (Lev. 17:11)

Lev. 17:11(a) tells us that the life of the flesh is in the blood.

This simply means that without the blood, in the flesh, there will be no life. This also mean spiritually and biologically that most of what you see the flesh do or experience is in the blood. Sicknesses, challenges, infirmities and behaviors can also be traceable to the blood.

Medical doctors use the blood frequently to check for sicknesses, diseases, infirmities and other genetic problems, even including a DNA check.

Just as your blood is used in the medical lab to investigate causes of diseases and sicknesses in your body, you also need to take your blood to the spiritual Lab and investigate what is causing you most of the spiritual problems and challenges you are faced with in life today.

The way people behave can also be scientifically detected by blood type and other means. Whenever doctors are investigating a cancer or diabetic patient, they do a background investigation of relatives who had such a medical challenge or history in their family, in order to know whether it is a blood issue in the family.

There are things we need to investigate spiritually to know if they are blood issues in the family also.

When Gehazi was cursed by Prophet Elisha in 2 Kings 5:21-27, every descendant of Gehazi that had leprosy could be traced to the blood of their ancestor Gehazi that was inside of them.

21 So Gehazi followed after Naaman. And when Naaman saw him running after him, he lighted down from the chariot to meet him, and said, Is all well?

22 And he said, All is well. My master hath sent me, saying, Behold, even now there be come to me from mount Ephraim two young men of the sons of the prophets: give them, I pray thee, a talent of silver, and two changes of garments.

23 And Naaman said, Be content, take two talents. And he urged him, and bound two talents of silver in two bags, with two changes of garments, and laid them upon two of his servants; and they bare them before him.

24 And when he came to the tower, he took them from their hand, and bestowed them in the house: and he let the men go, and they departed.

[25] But he went in, and stood before his master. And Elisha said unto him, Whence comest thou, Gehazi? And he said, Thy servant went no whither.

[26] And he said unto him, Went not mine heart with thee, when the man turned again from his chariot to meet thee? Is it a time to receive money, and to receive garments, and oliveyards, and vineyards, and sheep, and oxen, and menservants, and maidservants?

[27] The leprosy therefore of Naaman shall cleave unto thee, and unto thy seed forever. And he went out from his presence a leper as white as snow. (2 Kings 5:21-27)

Whatever is plaguing you today as a result of your ancestral or parental bloodline needs to be consciously neutralized by the blood of Jesus.

I want us to see the difference between a blood issue and an issue of blood. The story in Mark 5:25-34 explains to us an issue of blood.

[25] And a certain woman, which had an issue of blood twelve years,

[26] And had suffered many things of many physicians, and had spent all that she had, and was nothing bettered, but rather grew worse,

[27] When she had heard of Jesus, came in the press behind, and touched his garment.

[28] For she said, If I may touch but his clothes, I shall be whole.

[29] And straightway the fountain of her blood was dried up; and

she felt in her body that she was healed of that plague.

[30] And Jesus, immediately knowing in himself that virtue had gone out of him, turned him about in the press, and said, Who touched my clothes?

[31] And his disciples said unto him, Thou seest the multitude thronging thee, and sayest thou, Who touched me?

[32] And he looked round about to see her that had done this thing.

[33] But the woman fearing and trembling, knowing what was done in her, came and fell down before him, and told him all the truth.

[34] And he said unto her, Daughter, thy faith hath made thee whole; go in peace, and be whole of thy plague. (Mark 5:25-34)

An issue of blood is when you have an issue in your body that is causing you to bleed or causing a loss of blood.

This woman had an issue that was making her to bleed and she lost a lot of blood. The issue, medically , could be referred to as cancer of the uterus (womb) or cervical cancer. She was bleeding because she had an issue. But a blood issue is when you are carrying blood that is causing you a lot of issues.

[10] And he said, What hast thou done? the voice of thy brother's blood crieth unto me from the ground.

[11] And now art thou cursed from the earth, which hath opened her mouth to receive thy brother's blood from thy hand;

[12] When thou tillest the ground, it shall not henceforth yield unto thee her strength; a fugitive and a vagabond shalt thou be

in the earth.

[13] And Cain said unto the LORD, My punishment is greater than I can bear. (Genesis 4:10-13)

Jehovah was saying to Cain, in this passage of Scripture, you have brought upon yourself something more than you can ever imagine as a result of your brother's blood in your life.

Gen.4:10(a) And he said, what has thou done? This means, do you know the gravity of what you have brought upon yourself, by the blood of your brother, that has begun to cry in your life?

Do you know the level of setback and stagnation you have brought upon yourself, as the result of your brother's blood crying against you?

Do you know the level of struggle and limitation you have brought on yourself as a result of what you have done?

Do you understand the curse and hardship you have brought upon your life?

What has thou done? Do you know the power and weight of this blood issue?

If you had known, you wouldn't have done this, and you wouldn't have answered Me (JEHOVAH) the way you are doing.

Genesis 4:10(b) reveals to us that the blood has a voice. "The VOICE of thy brother's BLOOD crieth to me from the ground." This is how dangerous and serious a BLOOD ISSUE can be. The ground also opened its mouth, to cooperate with the blood, in order to place a curse and judgment upon Cain.

The blood has a voice and the ground has a mouth. They both

speak and work together on many occasions. Remember in the days of Moses, the ground opened its mouth and swallowed thousands.

²⁹ O earth, earth, earth, hear the word of the LORD.

³⁰ Thus saith the LORD, Write ye this man childless, a man that shall not prosper in his days: for no man of his seed shall prosper, sitting upon the throne of David, and ruling any more in Judah. (Jer. 22:29-30)

Jeremiah the Prophet recorded God's instruction to the earth to deal with a man and his generation.

²⁴ And to Jesus the mediator of the new covenant, and to the blood of sprinkling, that speaketh better things than that of Abel. (Hebrews 10:24).

The blood speaks.

This refers to the blood of Sprinkling, which is the blood of Jesus, that speaks better things than the blood of Abel. I want you to know that the blood speaks loudly and it speaks from generations to generations. The blood will continue to speak if the proper thing is not done, according to Scripture.

Gen. 4:12(a) When thou tiles the ground, it shall not henceforth yield unto thee her strength.

It is important for you to note that, before the blood issue, the ground was yielding its strength to Cain. And he was receiving a lot of produce and crops from the ground. But now God is saying to him that, because of the blood, his life will have issues, so much so, that the ground will not yield its strength and increase anymore to Cain. There are so many people struggling in life today, with different levels of talents, gifts, academic credentials, professions, beauty, eloquence and even good connections, but yet they cannot find their way out of struggle, poverty, setback, non-achievement, etc.

A blood issue is more destructive than an issue of blood. Issues of blood can cause you one thing which has to do with physical impairment. But a blood issue can cause a person so many challenges that cannot be numbered or easily diagnosed, if God doesn't help.

By the grace and help of the Lord, I will mention a few of them. Imagine, Cain was experienced, a super and fruitful farmer. But as a result of the blood issue, he became a failure. I wonder, how many people have been successful business men and women, ministers of the gospel and great politicians, and today have become failures in life, profession and ministry as a result of a blood issue?

Gen. 4:12(b) A fugitive and vagabond shall thou be in the earth.

Think about how many people are running around in the earth and don't even know from what they are running. They are going from one place to another, thinking that success or breakthrough is at the other location. When they get there, they find out that there is no difference in their case.

Some resort to all manner of improper things just to get out of their countries to western and developed countries, only to find out there is no change in their situation. Some people even relocate from America to Europe, from Europe to America, from Asia to Australia, from China to Japan, from South Korea to China, and still nothing has changed and the struggle continues. A blood issue has no respect for persons, race, color, nationality, or location.

Whenever there is a blood issue, there will be the same consequences and effects. It makes a person feel like there is no one in the entire world or universe to help him or her.

Blood issue affects people as a race, nation, family and as individuals. People around the world, without God's intervention, think and behave according to the blood inside of them. This is another aspect of blood issue to handle.

Please understand as I share a few examples. It is not my intention to offend, dishonor, or disrespect any race, nation or group of people. As a servant of God, it will never be and can never be my intention to do such. This is meant to only enlighten us to the blood issues.

Asians in general leave their country not seeking employment but to become employers. They go seeking opportunities for contracts for construction of roads, infrastructures, fishing industries, agriculture and self-employed businesses like restaurants, merchandise, etc.

By the grace of God, I've had the privilege of traveling to many nations around the world doing ministry, and this is what I have seen.

Some African Americans are very lazy and have a dependency syndrome.

African Americans have slavery in their history. This history creates a mentality of inferiority and dependency. This is a blood issue that keeps some from excelling, unless they break the curse of their culture.

Welfare has caused many African-American homes to be without fathers and disqualified them from many public positions and offices, except the few that are determined or carry another Spirit like Joshua and Caleb.

Africa has a similar problem among its people. Some hate knowledge and lack managerial abilities. That is the reason why the western nations are still dictating to our leaders and even determining who becomes president for many of our nations. Many Africans are earning academic degrees but not displaying the knowledge they have acquired. They seek education in the Western world. But you don't see that knowledge applied. That is why we are still lacking in development and management. The problem is these Africans' desire is not to seek knowledge. They are seeking academic titles and credentials rather than working knowledge.

Africa has all of the resources that are building all of the developed nations but never the headquarters of anything.

As one of the speakers at the Africa Transformation Conferences in Africa and to Africans in other continents, I have seen a lot. Another thing about Africans is that they seldom think about developing their continent but rather they line up at embassies of developed countries, seeking opportunity to migrate and do low-income jobs in other countries in the West and Asia. I mean very low-income jobs. None of the African countries is excluded.

Even our big shots, who have held governmental positions and honorable offices, they all go out there seeking migration and low-income jobs. The worst about it is that they steal money from our nations and store it in the western banks. And those nations use the money to build sky-high buildings; and in return, they loan us some of the same money and make us indebted to them.

This happens generation after generation, and it is never corrected or changed. Because, it is a blood issue with the Africans. Some Africans even die in deserts and oceans, trying to escape, when no one is pursuing them.

They escape to developed nations for better living, by doing jobs that citizens of those nations are not willing to do. One of the reasons is because many African leaders are not only unrighteous, but also bad and wicked managers.

Why is it that people in Europe, USA, Australia and China are not running to embassies or bypassing borders to enter into other countries? I want to prove this to you from the Bible. Egypt was a world Super Power in those days and yet couldn't manage their economy, even with a revelation from God. They had to give the nation over to a foreigner, Joseph from Israel, to manage the nation's economy for them.

Remember Egypt is in Africa. Joseph even helped Potiphar to prosper in Africa.

May God help deliver us and take this blood issue away in Jesus' name. When Americans are going into any nation, no matter what their undercover mission is, they are going there to help, even if it will profit them later. The least USA citizen, no matter which nation he or she travels to, never feels inferior or appears to be a beggar, even if he doesn't have much.

His government and people does not permit that. Because it is in their blood. It is in the blood of Americans to give and not look for help from outside.

Remember, I am not speaking from a political or social point of view. But I am saying these things because they are spiritually driven by the blood that is inside of these races, nations, and people.

I will also give you an example of a few nations in Africa, including my own nation Liberia.

Remember, nation is different from country. A country is a particular place where a group of people hails from. A nation is a group of people from a particular country, with a particular system and attitude no matter where they are.

Before I talk about these three nations from Africa, I want you to understand that the Jewish people are a nation from the country of Israel. Wherever they are, they think business, wealth, and development. Therefore, they are always counted amongst the wealthiest people amongst whom they reside.

Back to the three nations in Africa, specifically West Africa. Whenever Ghanians and Nigerians travel to any country in the world, they have a mentality and system of gathering wealth or getting something, in order to return home and build for themselves something great that will make them to be respected in their country and also help in development of the villages, cities and country.

In contrast, many Liberians would rather steal or take wealth from their country to go and establish themselves in other countries and help to develop those other countries. This has been an age-old problem and still continues today.

This is a blood issue which has to be settled by the blood of Jesus in order to help Liberia get to another level of development.

In every nation, there is something that is peculiar about certain tribes and people that are from different regions of that country.

Example: In Nigeria, the Yurobas are known as people who love to pursue higher education and carry a lot of degrees, the Igbos are people who are very popular for their business pursuits around the world, and the Hausas are known as people who love to deal with the military .

In Liberia, there are some things known about each tribe which I conclude to be a blood issue.

A few examples to give: the Kru tribe is known to be tough and aggressive people, Gola people are known to be people who do not release and are stingy, Gio people are known to be people who love too much power.

American Liberians, who are the settlers or called Congo people, are known to be selfish. Kpelleh people, because of their extreme humility, are considered to be foolish or stupid. Etc, etc, etc. This is true about many nations in the world and I could go on naming.

Study the life of the Native Americans and you will find out that there is a common warfare that they are fighting. Also check out the Aborigines of Australia; there is something common in them that they are struggling with, that makes them to live the life they are living in a nation to which they are natives.

We could continue this with many nations and peoples. This comes down to families and individuals that are confronted with all manner of issues, today.

Everything a man is confronted with in the area of infirmities, demonic troubles, bad habits like drunkenness, immoral lifestyle, divorce, inability to settle down in marriage, etc. can be traceable to blood issues.

Another Biblical example of the history of blood issue caused by bad blood is Lot and his family. When Lot and his daughters escaped divine judgment from Sodom and Gomorrah, they went up to a mountain to settle. There Lot's daughters made him drunk and committed incest with him and they each conceived and had a son.

One of the sons was Moab from whom Ruth descended (with an incest background) and went to Bethlehem and was married to Boaz (who was from a prostitute's background from Rahab of Jericho).

The both of them came together to give birth to Obed, who begat Jesse, who begat David also out of wedlock. David said he was conceived in iniquity (Psalm 51:5).

David also struggled with immorality by falling into adultery with Bathsheba, Uriah's wife, because of this blood issue. Because of the same blood issue, David's son Amnon raped his own sister, Tamar. And King Solomon took it to another level by having 700 wives and 300 concubines .

If you pay keen attention, you will discover that because of the blood issue, immorality in the form of incest, adultery and polygamy did not depart from this blood lineage.

There are habits and situations that so many people are struggling with today and have not been able to conquer because they are not cognizant of the fact that it is a result of a blood issue.

Until you discover, you cannot recover. Some results and consequences of blood issues are:

1. Failures in whatever you do where others succeed easily.

2. Bad luck and disappointments.

3. Troublesome children.

4. Generational infirmities and sicknesses.

5. Constant and frequent illnesses.

6. See-Saw life. (Today you are up and tomorrow you are down)

7. Frequent record of incest and adultery in the family line.

8. Inability to get married in the family line.

9. Long history of divorce in the family line.

10. Academic limitations.

11. Poverty and much more.

CHAPTER 6
DEMONIC COVERING (DRESS)

Demonic covering cast over you could be anything like a blanket, suit or garment that the enemy has dressed you with or covered you with in the realm of the spirit so that your glory cannot be seen.

There is spiritual dressing and physical dressing. Yet many are only aware of how they are dressed or arrayed in the natural realm and not concerned with how they are spiritually dressed.

To help us understand this, we need to check out what Apostle Paul says to us in Ephesians 6, speaking about spiritual warfare. He tells us to dress for warfare. This means you cannot go to fight in the spirit realm without dressing for war. Many have suffered and are suffering casualties because of not being properly dressed, attired, or arrayed for spiritual warfare.

Ephesians 6:10-17;

[10] Finally, my brethren, be strong in the Lord, and in the power of his might.

[11] Put on the whole armour of God, that ye may be able to stand against the wiles of the devil.

[12] For we wrestle not against flesh and blood, but against principalities, against powers, against the rulers of the darkness of this world, against spiritual wickedness in high places.

[13] Wherefore take unto you the whole armour of God, that ye may be able to withstand in the evil day, and having done all, to stand.

[14] Stand therefore, having your loins girt about with truth, and having on the breastplate of righteousness;

[15] And your feet shod with the preparation of the gospel of peace;

[16] Above all, taking the shield of faith, wherewith ye shall be able to quench all the fiery darts of the wicked.

[17] And take the helmet of salvation, and the sword of the Spirit, which is the word of God: (Ephesians 6:10-17)

I am sharing this in order for you to know that there is spiritual dressing.

Everything in the natural began from the spiritual. When God created man He dressed them spiritually with His Glory which covered them in the natural also, for they did not know that they were naked until the Devil came and removed their covering and they saw that they were naked.

Because of what they were covered with, they were protected, they were healthy, favored and attractive to good things so much that God could visit them at the cool of every day.

Can you imagine that? All because of how and what they were arrayed with, they enjoyed such privileges.

And when they lost the glory, they found and covered themselves with fig leaves which could not replace the glory.

You need to understand that the enemy is not only stealing the glory or garment that God gives us, but he is also putting onto his victims filthy garments that attract bad luck, disappointments, misfortunes, sicknesses and wrong partners in marital relationships. This could also lead to multiple divorces, wrong partners in business, etc. This causes great loss such as when Jonah made the business men to lose all their goods on the ship because Jonah was on the ship with them.

¹ And he shewed me Joshua the high priest standing before the angel of the LORD, and Satan standing at his right hand to resist him.

² And the LORD said unto Satan, The LORD rebuke thee, O Satan; even the LORD that hath chosen Jerusalem rebuke thee: is not this a brand plucked out of the fire?

³ Now Joshua was clothed with filthy garments, and stood before the angel.

4 And he answered and spake unto those that stood before him, saying, Take away the filthy garments from him. And unto him he said, Behold, I have caused thine iniquity to pass from thee, and I will clothe thee with change of raiment. (Zech. 3:1-4)

From the passage of Scripture above, you can see that Joshua was a high priest of God and faced lots of challenges with Satan at his right hand. Then God instructed the angel to change his filthy garments and put new garments on him.

As high priest, instead of attracting good things and the presence of God, he had Satan standing by his side because of the garment he had on.

With the many challenges he was confronted with, God recommended one solution, and that was to change his filthy garments. Because the spiritual garments he had on attracted all the wrong things in his life and brought the experience he had.

When the garments were changed, he could then exercise authority and function effectively as a high priest of God.

43 And when he thus had spoken , he cried with a loud voice, Lazarus, come forth.

44 And he that was dead came forth, bound hand and foot with grave clothes: and his face was bound about with a napkin. Jesus saith unto them, Loose him, and let him go. (John 11:43-44)

Lazarus came out of the grave, raised from the dead. This is similar to someone spiritually dead coming back to life by being born again.

Though he was born again, he was covered with grave clothes and a napkin all over his face. Though he was alive again, he was still covered with grave clothes which hid his appearance and kept him from living freely. Many people have come to Jesus and are saved but are still covered with demonic coverings (grave clothes).

When the grave cloth is upon someone, they can work so hard and yet people don't recognize their labor or appreciate them for anything. They can dress very well in the natural and never attract any one for marriage or a relationship. They can be qualified and yet not preferred for a job or promotion for any position. Sometimes they are hated without cause.

Grave clothes make people not to see you as they should.

It is the same as a covering that is cast and can manifest in the physical like a spider web covering you in very open places where others are walking freely. Sometimes you are walking with others and you are the only person feeling the touch of spider webs all over your face, while the others have no such experience.

Gen. 37:3-4;

³ Now Israel loved Joseph more than all his children, because he was the son of his old age: and he made him a coat of many colours.

⁴ And when his brethren saw that their father loved him more than all his brethren, they hated him, and could not speak peaceably unto him. (Gen. 37:3-4)

Gen. 39:3-6, 11-14;

³ And his master saw that the LORD was with him, and that the LORD made all that he did to prosper in his hand.

⁴ And Joseph found grace in his sight, and he served him: and he made him overseer over his house, and all that he had he put into his hand.

⁵ And it came to pass from the time that he had made him overseer in his house, and over all that he had, that the LORD blessed the Egyptian's house for Joseph's sake; and the blessing

of the LORD was upon all that he had in the house, and in the field.

[6] And he left all that he had in Joseph's hand; and he knew not ought he had, save the bread which he did eat. And Joseph was a goodly person, and well favoured. (Gen 39:3-6)

[11] And it came to pass about this time, that Joseph went into the house to do his business; and there was none of the men of the house there within.

[12] And she caught him by his garment, saying, Lie with me: and he left his garment in her hand, and fled, and got him out.

[13] And it came to pass, when she saw that he had left his garment in her hand, and was fled forth,

[14] That she called unto the men of her house, and spake unto them, saying, See, he hath brought in an Hebrew unto us to mock us; he came in unto me to lie with me, and I cried with a loud voice: (Gen. 39:11-14)

Gen. 41:39-43;

[39] And Pharaoh said unto Joseph, Forasmuch as God hath shewed thee all this, there is none so discreet and wise as thou art:

[40] Thou shalt be over my house, and according unto thy word shall all my people be ruled: only in the throne will I be greater than thou.

[41] And Pharaoh said unto Joseph, See, I have set thee over all the land of Egypt.

[42] And Pharaoh took off his ring from his hand, and put it upon Joseph's hand, and arrayed him in vestures of fine linen, and put a gold chain about his neck;

[43] And he made him to ride in the second chariot which he had; and they cried before him, Bow the knee: and he made him ruler over all the land of Egypt. (Gen. 41:39-43)

What I have discovered from these passages of Scripture is that several times people fought Joseph and took away his physical garments and tried to remove him from places of favor. But instead, he got new garments and higher favor than his previous position, because those who fought him had no knowledge of the spiritual garment he had on that attracted the physical garments and favor he was enjoying.

I want you to know that what you have on as a spiritual garment determines what you experience and enjoy in the natural. Whenever you are only attractive to unfavorable things in your life, you need to check how you are dressed spiritually.

Example: There are some men or women believing God for life partners, in order to settle down in life. But instead, only men and women who are already married and looking for sin partners are the ones attracted to them instead of single and serious individuals who are in search of spouses to marry.

You can destroy every covering by the fire of God, the blood of Jesus and the prayer of faith. Undress yourself from every demonic garment that by any means has been placed upon you.

You can also put on an attractive and glorious spiritual garment by faith using the Word of God to shield yourself daily with favor, cover yourself with glory, and declare that goodness and mercy are with you.

CHAPTER 7
TRANSFER OF VIRTUE

Success does not answer to family names, education, intelligence, beauty, etc., but rather, success answers to virtue.

VIRTUE RESTORATION

Mk. 5:25-34;

25 And a certain woman, which had an issue of blood twelve years,

26 And had suffered many things of many physicians, and had spent all that she had, and was nothing bettered, but rather grew worse,

27 When she had heard of Jesus, came in the press behind, and touched his garment.

28 For she said, If I may touch but his clothes, I shall be whole.

29 And straightway the fountain of her blood was dried up; and she felt in her body that she was healed of that plague.

30 And Jesus, immediately knowing in himself that VIRTUE had gone out of him, turned him about in the press, and said, Who touched my clothes?

31 And his disciples said unto him, Thou seest the multitude thronging thee, and sayest thou, Who touched me?

32 And he looked round about to see her that had done this thing.

33 But the woman fearing and trembling, knowing what was done in her, came and fell down before him, and told him all the truth.

34 And he said unto her, Daughter, thy faith hath made thee whole; go in peace, and be whole of thy plague. (Mark 5:25-34)

I discover from the passage of Scripture above that the lady with the issue of blood made frantic efforts to get a solution to her life-threatening health crisis, but to no avail. The reason was because the medical attention and all other efforts were not what she needed. Her condition did not only make her to bleed blood. The tradition and custom of those days did not allow a woman who was experiencing her monthly period or issue of blood to interact with people or be involved with public affairs. Therefore, she couldn't have relatives or friends interacting or getting involved with her in any way.

She bled friends and relatives out of her life. They all left her while she was bleeding blood. She also bled money. The Bible says she spent all that she had. What a terrible situation!

But I discovered that the reason she was bleeding everything out of her life was because her virtue had been taken away from her, which made her life unbearable and left her far from fulfilling destiny and experiencing joy. This is the reason why, when she touched the hem of the garment of Jesus, what was restored to her was virtue. And everything that had ever left her was restored. When virtue left Jesus and entered her she was made whole, meaning everything that had ever left her, including blood, relatives, friends, marriage, money, prestige, etc, was being restored by the restoration of her virtue.

Gen. 1:28;

[28] And God blessed them, and God said unto them, Be fruitful, and multiply, and replenish the earth, and subdue it: and have dominion over the fish of the sea, and over the fowl of the air, and over every living thing that moveth upon the earth. (Gen. 1:28)

In this context, 'be fruitful' means to *increase in quality* and 'multiply' means to *increase in quantity*. So God expects us to increase in quality before quantity.

The fruitful or quality aspect of the mandate or commission that God gave man had to do with virtue. Without virtue, there is no quality or ability to reproduce anything good.

SOME WAYS THAT VIRTUES ARE TRANSFERRED OR STOLEN

1. Physical sacrifice.

Physical sacrifice of virtue carriers on demonic altars or in covens and shrines has been done for centuries. These sacrifices are done in order for the victim's virtue to be passed on to those who seek virtue for increased power. An example of this is found in 2 Kings 3:25-27:

[25] And they beat down the cities, and on every good piece of land cast every man his stone, and filled it; and they stopped all the wells of water, and felled all the good trees: only in Kirharaseth left they the stones thereof; howbeit the slingers

went about it, and smote it.

²⁶ And when the king of Moab saw that the battle was too sore for him, he took with him seven hundred men that drew swords, to break through even unto the king of Edom: but they could not.

²⁷ Then he took his eldest son that should have reigned in his stead, and offered him for a burnt offering upon the wall. And there was great indignation against Israel: and they departed from him, and returned to their own land. (2 Kings 3:25-27)

When the king of Moab saw that his tenure was about to expire and he was about to be killed by the Israelites, he sacrificed his son (who had the virtue to take over as the next king) on a demonic altar, in order to transfer the virtue of the son to him the father for extension of his tenure.

2. Food.

¹ Now the serpent was more subtil than any beast of the field which the LORD God had made. And he said unto the woman, Yea, hath God said, Ye shall not eat of every tree of the garden?

² And the woman said unto the serpent, We may eat of the fruit of the trees of the garden:

³ But of the fruit of the tree which is in the midst of the garden, God hath said, Ye shall not eat of it, neither shall ye touch it, lest ye die.

⁴ And the serpent said unto the woman, Ye shall not surely die:

⁵ For God doth know that in the day ye eat thereof, then your eyes shall be opened, and ye shall be as gods, knowing good

and evil.

6 And when the woman saw that the tree was good for food, and that it was pleasant to the eyes, and a tree to be desired to make one wise, she took of the fruit thereof, and did eat, and gave also unto her husband with her; and he did eat.

7 And the eyes of them both were opened, and they knew that they were naked; and they sewed fig leaves together, and made themselves aprons. (Gen. 3:1-7)

Gen. 3:1-7; Adam and Eve lost everything after eating.

Your virtue is that glory, that power, that ability and force that God has given you to be all that God has called you to be, the power to fulfill divine purpose, accomplish your divine assignment, and be in charge here on the earth.

When Adam and Eve ate the fruit, the Bible says their eyes were opened and they knew that they were naked. This means they came to realization, they came to their senses like the prodigal son, and knew that the virtue that God had given to them which put them in charge had just left them after they had eaten.

They were clothed with glory but the glory departed after they ate the fruit.

They lost their dominion and Satan took over the earth they had been in charge of. And they became subject to the Devil.

They began to patch fig leaves for covering. They were looking for artificial or fake covering. Whenever people do not have virtue, they fake to survive and don't really live life as they should. That is why Jesus said He came that we may have life and have it in abundance. Because He came to restore the virtue that man lost to the Devil by Adam. Halleluiah!

Another example of virtue lost through the use of food is found in Dan. 1:1-9;

[1] In the third year of the reign of Jehoiakim king of Judah came Nebuchadnezzar king of Babylon unto Jerusalem, and besieged it.

[2] And the Lord gave Jehoiakim king of Judah into his hand, with part of the vessels of the house of God: which he carried into the land of Shinar to the house of his god; and he brought the vessels into the treasure house of his god.

[3] And the king spake unto Ashpenaz the master of his eunuchs, that he should bring certain of the children of Israel, and of the king's seed, and of the princes;

[4] Children in whom was no blemish, but well favoured, and skilful in all wisdom, and cunning in knowledge, and understanding science, and such as had ability in them to stand in the king's palace, and whom they might teach the learning and the tongue of the Chaldeans.

[5] And the king appointed them a daily provision of the king's meat, and of the wine which he drank: so nourishing them three years, that at the end thereof they might stand before the king.

[6] Now among these were of the children of Judah, Daniel, Hananiah, Mishael, and Azariah:

[7] Unto whom the prince of the eunuchs gave names: for he gave unto Daniel the name of Belteshazzar; and to Hananiah, of Shadrach; and to Mishael, of Meshach; and to Azariah, of Abednego.

⁸ But Daniel purposed in his heart that he would not defile himself with the portion of the king's meat, nor with the wine which he drank: therefore he requested of the prince of the eunuchs that he might not defile himself.

⁹ Now God had brought Daniel into favour and tender love with the prince of the eunuchs. (Dan. 1:1-9)

We can discover from the passage of Scripture above that the King of Babylon was interested in the virtues of the worthy children from Israel to enhance his kingdom and his kingly power and virtue.

Therefore he decided to use food to transfer the virtues of the worthy children of Israel to himself and render them useless. However, I want you to see that there were a certain four of the children of Israel that refused to defile themselves with the king's food.

If the food had had no special rituals done with it, why would they say: we will not defile ourselves with the king's food? If it didn't have power to defile or transfer virtues, why couldn't the king and his men feed everyone with the same food except those selected few and choice individuals?

Why is it that the rest of the royal children who ate the king's food, nothing was heard of them anymore? But rather only the certain four: Daniel, Shadrach, Meshach and Abednego were heard about continually. Even though they did not obey or submit to the laws of Babylon, they were the only Hebrews that attained higher heights and greater promotions at that time in the kingdom of Babylon.

They continued to reign and became indestructible, so much so that hungry, roaring lions could not eat them, nor could a blazing tempest fire consume them. Because they kept their virtue and the enemy could not take it away from them.

Be careful what you eat, where you eat and who you eat from. Because of their virtues, they remained people of solutions in the kingdom and the king could not do without them but rather depended on them for the greatness of his kingdom. Therefore, he kept exalting and promoting them above those who hated and opposed them.

3. Sex.

1 Cor. 6:16; [16] What? know ye not that he which is joined to an harlot is one body? for two, saith he, shall be one flesh. (1 Cor. 6:16)

One of the major ways that the enemy uses to rob people of their authority, power, glory and virtue is through sexual intercourse. Some people think they are lucky to sleep with big shots. There are many who think themselves so fortunate to be sleeping with people who are in authority or in high positions. But I want you to understand that sometimes the reason why people in authority or other high positions come to them is because they are using their victim's virtues to sustain themselves in those places or to attain higher heights.

This is why most secret cults and demonic societies encourage their clients and members who are seeking wealth, good living and higher positions to have sex with their own children or virgins in order to take away their virtues. When virtue is taken away from a person, no matter how hard they work they cannot achieve anything in life. They always end down at level zero in life.

When a man or woman sleeps with an agent seeking virtue, 50% of their virtue is shared with that person at the first time of sexual intercourse and the next time what is left will also be shared by 50% again and on and on. Later, when their virtue is depleted, they are told that they are bad luck and the relationship cannot continue. Frequently, the person who was receiving all of the good things in the relationship, when they find out that they have depleted all of their victim's virtue, suddenly quits the relationship. The victim begins to wonder why they are not calling, picking up their calls, visiting, and showing kindness anymore.

In Africa or within some cults, the victims are told that they are bad luck and need some rituals to be performed or baths to be done for them. When the victims are convinced or persuaded, because they are still interested in the assistance they think they are receiving, they accept and surrender to the evil practice. They then become victims and weapons for the occultist at another level. After the ritual is done, the occultist uses them as agents to have sexual intercourse with others, and in this way collect the virtues of the people they have sexual relationships with in order to transfer it to the occultist or the agent.

So if you want to fulfill your destiny, you will have to be careful and not have sexual intercourse with just anyone anywhere. If you do, you might end up losing your virtue, struggle for the rest of your life, and not fulfill your destiny or your divine purpose.

I have seen girls, who were so beautiful and bright (smart), sleep with some so-called big shots and they lost their virtue. As a result of that, their glory and beauty departed from them.

They were no longer attractive and they became the lowest of the lowest. Some of them had driven the best of cars, lived in nice apartments, traveled to the best of places and handled great sums of money. But today, they are living as if they had never seen anything like that. The simple reason is that without virtue, you lack the authority, ability and capacity to command and attract the things needed to fulfill destiny or your divine purpose.

E.g. Joseph and Mrs. Potiphar

[6] And he left all that he had in Joseph's hand; and he knew not ought he had, save the bread which he did eat. And Joseph was a goodly person, and well favoured.

[7] And it came to pass after these things, that his master's wife cast her eyes upon Joseph; and she said, Lie with me.

[8] But he refused, and said unto his master's wife, Behold, my master wotteth not what is with me in the house, and he hath committed all that he hath to my hand;

[9] There is none greater in this house than I; neither hath he kept back anything from me but thee, because thou art his wife: how then can I do this great wickedness, and sin against God?

[10] And it came to pass, as she spake to Joseph day by day, that he hearkened not unto her, to lie by her, or to be with her.

[11] And it came to pass about this time, that Joseph went into the house to do his business; and there was none of the men of the house there within.

[12] And she caught him by his garment, saying, Lie with me: and he left his garment in her hand, and fled, and got him out. (Gen.

39:6-12)

Joseph knew he had a destiny to fulfill. He knew he had a divine purpose to fulfill on the earth and also in his family. Therefore he refused to sleep or have any form of sexual relationship with Mrs. Potiphar because she was a virtue-snatcher and a destiny-amputator. She could not stand the fact that Joseph came, met everyone in that empire, and became the shining star and boss and took charge of everything, even in her presence. She knew that he was not ordinary and was carrying great virtue, so she tried to seize and hijack it through sexual intercourse.

If Joseph had surrendered to her, he would have lost everything and Potiphar's house would have been his highest height. But because he refused and rejected her devilish and demonic offers to exchange his virtue for the temporary pleasure of sex, he attained a great height in the nation of Egypt and in the earth at that time. He also fulfilled his God-given dream of his family bowing before him and also his divine purpose of sustaining the great nation of Egypt and the other nations of the earth in the time of horrible famine .

Why do you think a man or a woman is willing to give a boy or a girl so much, just for sex? The moment they leave, everything with them is gone. I want you to understand that the reason is because they are taking from that person more than what they promise or give to them. The virtue they are transferring from you can produce more than what they are giving you, at that moment.

If it is for the sake of just having sex, why don't they go pay the beautiful loose girls or sexy prostitutes out there less money without stress and have sex with them? They'd rather come and pay so much to you, just for one moment. Think about it.

If it was just for the case of wickedness, why don't the diabolic and demonic politicians who practice occultism kill or murder the crazy (mentally-deranged) or homeless people who are in the street but instead come after the lives of people who have substance, virtue, and focus in life?

This is to let you know that they have a target and they are aiming at people with virtues for greatness.

Homosexuality, which has to do with gay men and lesbianism, is not natural and is abnormal.

It is not a natural thing or feeling for a man to reject and have no affection for a woman and desire another man like himself. This is not only against the will and Word of God, but highly demonic. How much more so, when so many women are around. A man is willing to spend so much money, offer a car, and high positions in so many world-class institutions and government just to have sex with another man like himself. And people are thinking that it is ordinary.

Think about so many men around (even promiscuous ones seeking for any woman to have sex with) and there are women willing to offer so much money, elegant cars, high positions to other women in order to have sexual relations with them even for just one time. This is also abnormal and unnatural. But this is all because they take away more than they give.

Many times people don't know and understand the deep things of the occult and secret societies, and so all they think about is pleasure, wealth, or positions.

I want you to know this day, that there is more to what you see and know on the surface. Whenever such things are going on, virtues are being tampered with and transferred. Many people have lost their great destinies and missed out on their divine purposes because of temporary pleasures.

[21] Because that, when they knew God, they glorified him not as God, neither were thankful; but became vain in their imaginations, and their foolish heart was darkened.

[22] Professing themselves to be wise, they became fools,

[23] And changed the glory of the uncorruptible God into an image made like to corruptible man, and to birds, and four-footed beasts, and creeping things.

[24] Wherefore God also gave them up to uncleanness through the lusts of their own hearts, to dishonour their own bodies between themselves:

[25] Who changed the truth of God into a lie, and worshipped and served the creature more than the Creator, who is blessed forever. Amen.

[26] For this cause God gave them up unto vile affections: for even their women did change the natural use into that which is against nature:

[27] And likewise also the men, leaving the natural use of the woman, burned in their lust one toward another; men with men working that which is unseemly, and receiving in themselves that recompense of their error which was meet.

[28] And even as they did not like to retain God in their knowledge, God gave them over to a reprobate mind, to do those things which are not convenient; (Rom. 1:21-28)

4. Exchange of Garments.

As spiritual people, we need to be careful of the people we interact with and with whom we share our things. Because the world today is evil and you may not know the hearts of the people around you.

[9] The heart is deceitful above all things, and desperately wicked: who can know it? (Jer. 17:9)

Your clothes carry your sweat and odor. Therefore it is easy for it to be used to manipulate your destiny, health, and many other things about you. You need to understand that your sweat comes out of your blood and the life of the flesh is in the blood (Lev. 17:11). I want you to know also that even Jesus, as much as He wanted many souls into the kingdom while He walked here on the earth, He was very careful with people who came into His fold.

[24] But Jesus did not commit himself unto them, because he knew all men. (John 2:24)

Jesus is our perfect example and so you cannot be holier than Him. Be careful with whom you share your personal space and personal things.

5. Demonic dedications and baths.

Some who are suffering today did not start now. It began when the mother and/or father turned them over to their unknown or secret enemies to dedicate them. They may have bathed them or named them. In the process, those wicked people can exchange the virtue of the child by performing rituals that are not Godly or righteous. They use that time also to make incantations and place curses on the infants. Sometimes, while bathing them, they wash away blessings and every good thing that they discover by their mediums. Therefore, don't trust everyone with your children and babies. Children are meant to be taken care of by their parents, not grandparents or any others, in order for their virtues to be sustained or protected. They are vulnerable at that tender age to every attack of the enemy.

6. Demonic embraces and laying on of hands.

Every child of God needs to pray for the gift and spirit of discernment, because there are agents of darkness who come in disguise to God's house to accomplish missions of their master. Some of them are even posing as pastors, prophets or carrying some kind of apostolic title. They lay hands on people which can take people into the realm of darkness and cause complex problems in their lives. We need to be careful to maintain our blessings and breakthrough that God has given and promised us. Many times when you embrace people, they either extract something from you or add something to you. The same is true in the laying on of hands.

CHAPTER 8
DEMONIC DEDICATIONS

THE FUNDAMENTALS OF A DEDICATION

In order to identify demonic dedications, let us study an example of a Godly dedication.

Lk. 2:20-40;

20 And the shepherds returned, glorifying and praising God for all the things that they had heard and seen, as it was told unto them.

21 And when eight days were accomplished for the circumcising of the child, his name was called JESUS, which was so named of the angel before he was conceived in the womb.

22 And when the days of her purification according to the law of Moses were accomplished, they brought him to Jerusalem, to present him to the Lord;

23 (As it is written in the law of the Lord, Every male that openeth the womb shall be called holy to the Lord;)

24 And to offer a sacrifice according to that which is said in the law of the Lord, a pair of turtledoves, or two young pigeons.

²⁵ And, behold, there was a man in Jerusalem, whose name was Simeon; and the same man was just and devout, waiting for the consolation of Israel: and the Holy Ghost was upon him.

²⁶ And it was revealed unto him by the Holy Ghost, that he should not see death, before he had seen the Lord's Christ.

²⁷ And he came by the Spirit into the temple: and when the parents brought in the child Jesus, to do for him after the custom of the law,

²⁸ Then took he him up in his arms, and blessed God, and said,

²⁹ Lord, now lettest thou thy servant depart in peace, according to thy word:

³⁰ For mine eyes have seen thy salvation,

³¹ Which thou hast prepared before the face of all people;

³² A light to lighten the Gentiles, and the glory of thy people Israel.

³³ And Joseph and his mother marveled at those things which were spoken of him.

³⁴ And Simeon blessed them, and said unto Mary his mother, Behold, this child is set for the fall and rising again of many in Israel; and for a sign which shall be spoken against;

³⁵ (Yea, a sword shall pierce through thy own soul also,) that the thoughts of many hearts may be revealed.

³⁶ And there was one Anna, a prophetess, the daughter of Phanuel, of the tribe of Aser: she was of a great age, and had lived with an husband seven years from her virginity;

[37] And she was a widow of about fourscore and four years, which departed not from the temple, but served God with fastings and prayers night and day.

[38] And she coming in that instant gave thanks likewise unto the Lord, and spake of him to all them that looked for redemption in Jerusalem.

[39] And when they had performed all things according to the law of the Lord, they returned into Galilee, to their own city Nazareth.

[40] And the child grew, and waxed strong in spirit, filled with wisdom: and the grace of God was upon him. (Luke 2:20-40)

This is a biblical example of Godly dedication. V:22 says, And when the days of her purification according to the law of Moses were accomplished, they brought him to Jerusalem, to present him to the Lord;

The child was taken to a place to be presented to the Lord.

After your birth, where did they take you? To whom did they take you? And to whom did they dedicate or present you?

Whether consciously or unconsciously, every child that is born is taken to a place or somebody who presents them to somebody or something and speaks something over his/her life.

When you find out that the life you are living does not look like your destiny, your vision or what your dream or purpose is or should be, you need to investigate.

You need to find out: where were you born? How were you born? Where were you taken after birth and to whom? And also who was it that did your dedication and to what or whom were you dedicated? This is very important because it helps to shape your life and direct the course of your life.

Lk. 2:23-24;

[23] (As it is written in the law of the Lord, Every male that openeth the womb shall be called holy to the Lord;)

[24] And to offer a sacrifice according to that which is said in the law of the Lord, A pair of turtledoves, or two young pigeons.

We discover from this passage of Scripture that Jesus, as a child, was brought to the temple according to the custom that His parents belonged to and practiced. Because it was of the Lord, the Bible says that a sacrifice was made according to the laws of the Lord.

Ask yourself, which customs did my parents practice at the time of my birth and which secret society were they a part of? What law and sacrifice did they use to dedicate me?

Since then, what kind of influence am I under? Many people have been dedicated according to the Freemason pattern and principles or some other occult group.

In Africa and Asia, there are many cultures and backgrounds that have linked people to millions of deities and practices that are contrary to God's purpose and these are used to dedicate children.

This is one of the reasons why millions of people from such places and backgrounds spent 75 percent of their lives struggling before they can discover their destiny and begin to pursue it.

Whatever a person or thing is dedicated to is what influences and dictates the course of that person or thing.

THE CHARACTERISTICS AND ASSIGNMENT OF THE PRIEST

[25] And, behold, there was a man in Jerusalem, whose name was Simeon; and the same man was just and devout, waiting for the consolation of Israel: and the Holy Ghost was upon him.

[26] And it was revealed unto him by the Holy Ghost, that he should not see death, before he had seen the Lord's Christ.

[27] And he came by the Spirit into the temple: and when the parents brought in the child Jesus, to do for him after the custom of the law, (LK. 2:25-27)

Remember, this man Simeon was just and devout according to the laws of God. He did not love anything or partake in any practices that were contrary to the laws of God. He had right standing with God.

He was waiting for the consolation of Israel. He had an assignment to the nation. The dedication of Jesus was the fulfillment of his assignment to the nation of Israel.

And the Holy Ghost was upon him for the assignment.

V:26; He had a revelation of his assignment that was connected to what the angel had said to Mary about herself and the destiny of the Child, that He would be the Savior of His people.

V:27; when the parents brought the Child according to the custom, he 'came by the Spirit'.

His role was divinely influenced and orchestrated.

What are the characteristics of the priest who dedicated you? Was he godly-qualified or demonically-prepared to dedicate you?

What spirit was upon him? Because the Holy Ghost was upon Simeon.

What voice had he been hearing? The Holy Ghost spoke to Simeon.

Simeon came by the Spirit of God into the temple. What spirit influenced the priest who dedicated you?

The unction a man is under to function determines who or what is in charge of the occasion.

What is the assignment of the priest? Who is he working for? And that will influence your life.

THE POWER OF WORDS IN DEDICATION

Lk. 2:28-39;

28 Then took he him up in his arms, and blessed God, and said,

29 Lord, now lettest thou thy servant depart in peace, according to thy word:

30 For mine eyes have seen thy salvation,

31 Which thou hast prepared before the face of all people;

32 A light to lighten the Gentiles, and the glory of thy people Israel.

33 And Joseph and his mother marveled at those things which were spoken of him.

³⁴ And Simeon blessed them, and said unto Mary his mother, Behold, this child is set for the fall and rising again of many in Israel; and for a sign which shall be spoken against;

³⁵ (Yea, a sword shall pierce through thy own soul also,) that the thoughts of many hearts may be revealed.

³⁶ And there was one Anna, a prophetess, the daughter of Phanuel, of the tribe of Aser: she was of a great age, and had lived with an husband seven years from her virginity;

³⁷ And she was a widow of about fourscore and four years, which departed not from the temple, but served God with fastings and prayers night and day.

³⁸ And she coming in that instant gave thanks likewise unto the Lord, and spake of him to all them that looked for redemption in Jerusalem.

³⁹ And when they had performed all things according to the law of the Lord, they returned into Galilee, to their own city Nazareth. (Lk. 2:28-39)

V:28; Simeon blessed the name of the Lord. Who did they exalt when they were dedicating you?

Who and what was in the mind of the priest?

VV:29-33; The Priest Simeon spoke prophetic words concerning Jesus.

He was declaring and confirming what God had already decided for Jesus and His mother. This pertained to how He would be a light to the Gentiles and for the falling and rising of many in

Israel and how, because of what He would go through, His mother would feel like a sword had pierced her soul.

He declared what God had determined for the Child Jesus. And that is what dedication is all about: to declare and to proclaim and confirm God's purpose for a person or thing. Dedication is also meant for reinforming what God has determined, like what Simeon did concerning Jesus.

Your dedication was prophetic words released over your life to guide and lead you to your divine destiny.

But when a demonic dedication is done with a person, it drives them away from their God-given destiny, keeping them from fulfilling divine purpose.

Example: Gen. 25:20-26;

20 And Isaac was forty years old when he took Rebekah to wife, the daughter of Bethuel the Syrian of Padanaram, the sister to Laban the Syrian.

21 And Isaac intreated the LORD for his wife, because she was barren: and the LORD was intreated of him, and Rebekah his wife conceived.

22 And the children struggled together within her; and she said, If it be so, why am I thus? And she went to enquire of the LORD.

23 And the LORD said unto her, Two nations are in thy womb, and two manner of people shall be separated from thy bowels; and the one people shall be stronger than the other people; and the elder shall serve the younger.

²⁴ And when her days to be delivered were fulfilled, behold, there were twins in her womb.

²⁵ And the first came out red, all over like an hairy garment; and they called his name Esau.

²⁶ And after that came his brother out, and his hand took hold on Esau's heel; and his name was called Jacob: and Isaac was threescore years old when she bare them.

Isaac entreated the Lord and his prayers were answered. You are aware that when God answers your prayer, He gives you a better answer to your prayers than what you asked for. And so the Lord answered Isaac with double instead of single. And not only that, instead of ordinary children, he gave them nations.

V:23; God spoke to Rebekah about the destiny of the children.

V:26; The younger one was dedicated according to his behavior at birth and his parents' feelings, not according to his destiny. For that reason his life was miserable for years and even for a generation.

The name Jacob that was given to him at dedication was contrary to God's purpose of greatness and fulfillment in his life. So he struggled for everything he was entitled to for years and was even about to be assassinated by his brother, until God intervened when he encountered the angel and was rededicated with his new name Israel.

Remember, Esau was looking for Jacob to kill him. But then, when they met, he had already been dedicated as Israel and so the plan to assassinate him was aborted.

Many people are suffering many things and are victims in life, marriage, business, etc. because of wrong and demonic dedications.

The kind of dedication done for you can deliver you from evil and establish you in divine purpose.

OUTCOME OF JESUS' DEDICATION

Luke 2:40;

40 And the child grew, and waxed strong in spirit, filled with wisdom: and the grace of God was upon him.

All this happened because of the characteristic of the priest and the godly dedication that was done in line with His destiny and divine purpose.

The name that was used in dedication was so correct that even Anna, the widow in the temple, came in to confirm His assignment of redemption.

Luke 2:33;

33 And Joseph and His mother marveled at those things which were spoken of Him. (Lk. 2:33)

The parents of Jesus were astonished at what the Priest Simeon spoke because it was confirmation of what the Lord had already spoken to them.

Investigate your dedication. And if it was a wrong one, you need to do a new dedication with your name and the purpose you have discovered.

CHAPTER 9
PRAYERS OF DELIVERANCE

As Abraham made a good and positive covenant with God that is affecting our lives today, I want you to pray and break, using the blood of Jesus, every evil covenant that your ancestors or parents made with evil spirits affecting your life and destiny.

Pray and say:

I break the power of every evil covenant that was made on my behalf, or by me, consciously or unconsciously, with any demonic spirit, fetish priest, occultist, open societies, secret societies and any agent of darkness in any place at any time, that is ruining my life and destiny, causing setbacks, disappointments, infirmities and constant failures in my life, in Jesus' mighty name and by the power of the blood of Jesus Christ of Nazareth.

With the blood of Jesus, I break the power of every witchcraft and demonic curse working against my life and destiny.

In the name of Jesus, I revoke and renounce every negative word and every evil or negative pronouncement speaking against me from any demonic altar or evil priest.

I withdraw my spirit, soul, and body from every evil dedication that was done with my life at any time and any place. I consecrate my entire being with the blood of Jesus Christ and declare: I have been purchased by the blood of Jesus Christ and I belong to Him and Him only.

I withdraw my virtue and my star that represent my destiny from every coven, shrine and demonic altar from which evil agents are monitoring and manipulating my destiny.

In Jesus' mighty name, I release the fire of God to destroy everything they are using to represent me in those evil places.

I declare, by the truth and knowledge of God's Word and the liberty that is in Christ Jesus, I am delivered and free from every demonic bondage, in the mighty righteous and holy name of Jesus Christ, the holy Son of God.

Shout and say, "I am free in Jesus' name!", 7 times.

CONCLUSION

I want every believer in Jesus Christ to know that the strongest giant tormenting your life and holding you captive is not the Devil, but your lack of knowledge of God's Word and your failure to crave and desire God's engrafted Word above everything you have ever desired in life.

Cleave to God's Word and consider it above every situation you face. Then your freedom will be certain.

ABOUT THE AUTHOR

Bishop John Kun Kun is the senior pastor of the City of Light Church of God in Barnersville Estate, Monrovia, Liberia since 1998.

He is a former Administrative Bishop and Missionary of the Church of God in Sierra Leone and Republic of Guinea from 2006-2010 and the Republic of Mali from 2010-2014.

Currently Bishop Kun Kun is the president of the Liberia Fellowship of Full Gospel Ministers and Ministries with the oversight of nearly 3,000 churches since 2014.

He is also the Second Vice President of the Haven of Rest Ministers Network (headquartered in South Africa). And he also serves as International Coordinator for Jesus Global Harvest Ministries (headquartered in Abuja, Nigeria).

Bishop is an international speaker at the Africa Transformation Conferences. He is a conference, revival, crusade, radio and television speaker. He ministers in many places around the world, including Africa, Europe, Australia, the United States and China.

The anointing and power of God for signs and wonders, healings, deliverance and transformation is always present when the Word of God is preached. Many men and women from criminal and demonic backgrounds have been impacted by his ministry, including the notorious former General Butt Naked (a Liberian rebel fighter) who is now converted to Evangelist Joshua Milton Blahyi.   Bishop Kun Kun is married to Prophetess/Pastor Yvonne Kun and blessed with three beautiful daughters, grandchildren and countless spiritual children around the world. To God be all the glory.

Made in the USA
Lexington, KY
29 December 2018